UNIVERSAL PRIMER

ANCIENT WISDOM THROUGH MODERN EYES:
A GUIDE TO UNIVERSAL LAWS AND TIMELESS TRUTHS

GALEN STOLLER

EDITED BY K PAUL STOLLER, MD

Universal Primer: A Guide to Universal Laws and Timeless Truths
Copyright © 2025 by K. Paul Stoller

For more about this author please visit https://www.dreamtreaderpress.com/

This author is not engaged in rendering medical or psychological services, and this book is not intended as a guide to diagnose or treat medical or psychological problems. If you require medical, psychological, or other expert assistance, please seek the services of your own physician or mental health professional.

All rights reserved. No part of this publication may be reproduced, distributed, or transmitted in any form or by any means, including photocopying, recording, or other electronic or mechanical methods, without the prior written permission of the author, except in the case of brief quotations embodied in critical reviews and certain other noncommercial uses permitted by copyright law. Please do not participate in or encourage piracy of copyrighted materials in violation of the author's rights.

No part of this book may be used for the training of artificial systems, including systems based on artificial intelligence (AI), without the copyright owner's prior permission. This prohibition shall be in force even on platforms and systems that claim to have such rights based on an implied contract for hosting the book.

Paperback ISBN: 978-0-9882027-8-8
Hardcover ISBN: 978-0-9882027-7-1

1. Main category—Religion & Spirituality › Spirituality › Personal Growth › Transformational
2. Other category—Religion & Spirituality › New Age › Channeling
3. Other category—Religion & Spirituality › New Age › Self-Help

Published by: Dream Treader Press
K. Paul Stoller, Publisher
DreamTreaderPress.com
With American Real Publishing
americanrealpublishing.com

TABLE OF CONTENTS

Prologue ... 1
PART I ... 11
   The First Universal Law – Cause and Effect ... 13
   The Law of Manifestation ... 23
   The Law of Attraction ... 29
   The Law of Rhythm ... 37
   The Law of Vibration ... 45
   The Law of Gender ... 51
   The Law of Universal Mind ... 57
   The Law of No Separation ... 67
Part II ... 75
   The Universal Keys ... 76
   Temperance ... 77

The Crossroads	80
The Connection	83
The Decision	87
The Trust	91
The Joy	94
The Journey	96
The Beginning and the End	98
About the Author	101
About the Editor	102

*You will travel far, my little Kal-El.
But we will never leave you...
even in the face of our deaths.
You will make my strength your own.
See my life through your own eyes,
as your life will be seen through mine.
The son becomes the father,
and the father...the son.*

—Jor-El (Marlon Brando 1978, *Superman*)

PROLOGUE

THE UNIVERSAL PRIMER IS THE ABCs of what being in a human body on earth is energetically all about. It is that simple. This primer was a project I originally started with the birth of my son, Galen; I wanted to have a guidebook for him so he could understand the ancient wisdom and how it applied to our current day. I spent two years gathering the material I wanted to include in this guide, and then I started writing it. It was never published, and Galen never read it, although I read him sections from time to time. Virtually nothing of that effort made it into the version you have before you, except in so much as it was training for me so when I received the material that became this primer, I would know something of what I was writing. What irony that Galen would turn around and present me with a universal guide—the universal laws and truths[1] that he has now come to revere and wants to share for the benefit of all those who turn these pages.

---

1 Truths exist in the lower realms, such as the third dimension. Truth is a perception of an idea that resonates.

Galen would have been twenty-one years old during the year (2012) he presented this material, had he remained on earth. When I told him how much time had passed since he was struck by a train at the end of 2007, he was taken aback, because there is no linear time in his dimension, and his perception of his life now was that decades had gone by. Galen has a lot to share about his sojourn on the other side, and I encourage those who are interested to read his *Death Walker* book series that starts with his first book, *My Life after Life*. However, this book is not about Galen and his story or my story.[2]

In fact, Galen wants it known, "*In no ways or means am I this enlightened or bright about every single law of the universe, so this is also a collaboration with teachers and on a greater scale with others. I have a very small part in this in the context of comment—these are the things that are taught over and over in the understanding of my own experiences, and because it has helped me a great deal, it shall help others. And to have this information before one leaves their earth body, rather than waiting till one arrives (on the other side), was something I wanted to assist in its creation.*"

Galen laughed and told me there would be comments from the "peanut gallery."

---

[2] Galen would have been heading off to his senior year in college in 2012, and maybe I would be barely seeing him, or even talking to him. Maybe we wouldn't be on good terms. None of this matters—what matters is that your humble scribe is still very human, and some days are good, and some days are not. Only a parent who has lost a child knows what I am talking about. I did not write this in blood, but there were a thousand tears for every word in this primer—enough said.

Even before Galen provided the information that became his first book, *My Life After Life,* I irreverently called the many unknown and unseen observers of my earthly travail *the peanut gallery,* after the group of children who would watch the Howdy Doody puppet perform in the classic 1950s TV show. Sometimes I would hear them comment about my dreamtime activities, which was not unlike the experience Billy Pilgrim (the Kurt Vonnegut Jr. character from the book *Slaughterhouse-Five*) had when the alien race, the Tralfamadorians, kidnapped him and put him in a zoo. But we don't have to go to some imaginary planet to be in a zoo.

As beautiful as I think our planet is, and as necessary as it may be to understand the polarity of the third dimension, it seems to be a bit of a zoo to me, and perhaps that is my cynical side coming through, because others would call it a spiritual classroom. I wish I could be that neutral. That may be my personality's perception, and I will admit I am jaded, so it doesn't have to be yours. I have said this here in the prologue, so it hopefully won't filter through anywhere else in this primer. Nevertheless, I am honored to be part of this collaboration as well and join with those who are in service to help bring forward the ancient wisdom of universal laws and truths. Many have stepped forward to create this guide because it is a universal primer—the ABCs of alignment with the energies we work with as humans and beyond.

And when I say many have stepped forward, I am obviously including those who have been able to reach me in dreams and other means, for I have made myself open to receive information outside the normal avenues available on third dimensional earth, not because I want to be a mystic, philosopher, or teacher. For me, this has always been about connecting with my son and working with him, and he wanted this primer to be available for others. I am just making this happen for him with as much integrity as possible, because he can't be here to do that for himself. I am his representative on earth at the moment. I am disclosing that this is my agenda. I do not need to go into detail about this, but I do not require any attention drawn to myself, nor do I seek it out. I have dedicated my professional life to bringing knowledge of hyperbaric medicine to the fore and how it can help brain-injured children and adults. This primer and Galen's *Death Walker* series do not advance my credibility in that area, so understand that there is some reluctance I have in my involvement here. But family comes first with me, and Galen wants this information available to earth's residents.

First and foremost, I think it is important to establish exactly what universal laws and truths are. They are descriptions of structures and paradigms that move through the universe, not just the physical material universe, although, stars, nebula, and galaxies certainly represent some of this information. Galen wanted to be clear that his use of the word *universe* in this context can be interchangeable with *Source* or *God*—it can replace the phrase *All That Is* or *Mother, Father Sky*. In other words, the universe is a form, but more than just the physicality of that form. So this is about energy and how that energy responds to all the multiple manifestations of that form in this universe—the thread of truth through everything in our benevolent universe.[3]

Benevolence is about love, compassion, and connectedness, and our universe holds these qualities. But a benevolent universe is where energy radiates outwardly and expansively. It is about giving—a benevolent universe gives out a radiance of energy. Since spirit and Source are neutral, it does not seem that the radiance of our universe is a kindness. But a central source of energy that radiates outwardly is just that. The opposite of a benevolent universe is where all form and energy are compacted into a central core and compressed, creating pressure and change. Everything feels disconnected and chaotic. Imagine the difference between a young star and a black hole, but on a much larger scale. The radiance of a benevolent universe becomes something where the compression of a malevolent universe becomes nothing.

On earth these two forces of nature are experienced through the polarity present in our dimension, but neither force is emitting a true form of itself. On earth, these polar opposite forces are so stepped down that we experience only the flavor of what true benevolence or true malevolence is actually like. Only the illusion of these forces can exist in the same space—the real nature of these forces cannot be present together; any more than matter and antimatter can be present in the same space. At any given moment the flavor of these forces on earth may exist in

---

[3] There are a multitude of universes, and each one operates under its own laws and truths.

a 50/50 ratio, but if true benevolence were unleashed on our planet, it would be impossible for polarity to be present, as this reality would completely overwhelm the earth paradigm. Conversely, if true malevolence were unleashed on earth, the planet would be consumed and dissipate. So that is why the earth is so unique, because at any given moment, joy, fear, compassion, cruelty, connectedness, or disconnectedness are available to experience, and it is by the choice of recognition that one or the other of these fields gets experienced. By our frame of mind, we make the day or what we determine it to be. Because earth exists in a benevolent universe, much of what takes place on earth is about radiance, it is easy to create here, but still there is the illusion of shadow, the illusion of that which compresses and destroys, and many get locked into that.

It is one's free will and choice to side with love or with fear; just understand that fear is not how things actually work beyond the classroom container of earth (or other earth-like dimensions). It is like having the choice to swim upstream (fear) or downstream (love)—not really a choice at all, when you understand all the implications, but a choice nevertheless. So, either you are radiating or you are contracting. Yet, this universal primer is not about how energy circulates in a macro-cosmic sense in our great multiverse. This primer is about how energy is integrated into the coalescence of form that is us, human beings, and how it operates with us.

Now, even though each individual will interpret universal law and truth (and energy) through their own belief systems, this collaboration will focus on the very primary ones. But Galen also wanted it understood why this project has come around now. This is not just another project between father and son,[4] but as this is a time of a great shift and change (not in any of the universal laws and truths), by understanding them there will be assistance with the evolution that is now taking place on earth. Certainly, each of us on earth is paying attention to what is happening around us on our planet, but there is also a greater shift and change that is taking place with the being who is the earth[5] and the solar system to which the earth belongs.

Much like the chakra system, which can be viewed as an energetic ladder of operational transducers, man is moving into the age of the heart chakra (and leaving the age of the solar plexus). But the forces that are making this profound shift possible also place the earth into a different vibration. That new vibration emits out into the energy field of the universe. So, to quote Galen, *"This is a Big Deal what is happening on earth!"*

The emphasis that Galen has just pointed out is also the emphasis of this collaboration (group, consensus, committee—but calling them the peanut gallery does not do them justice), along with its desire to assist those who

---

4 On a personal note, my gratitude for being able to have a connection with my son, and for us to do something that has the potential to be of service to others is beyond words. My grief was so intense after Galen passed that it would be no exaggeration to say I would have crossed over myself in short order if this bridge between us had not been created.

5 The earth is a conscious being on a grand scale.

need this information for a wider understanding. Even though this material has been taught for eons in human experience, Galen said, "Sometimes the old teachings are the best—the old-school way." And he wants others to know that there are steps to becoming awake, but he does not like to use the word enlightenment, because we are all born enlightened. Remembering how we became enlightened is part of what understanding universal laws and truths is all about.

While this can all sound very airy-fairy or new-age, and I mean that in the most pejorative sense, I want to point out why this information is relevant to the understanding of self and the understanding of life itself. There are four forces that are known to exist in our universe: electromagnetic, weak and strong nuclear, and gravity. There is a fifth force that is all-encompassing and is the source of all things and no things all at the same time, and while it would be far too easy to drift into some Jedi knight Yoda'ism, this force, as it manifests from light to color, sound, geometric form, and archetypes (as it comes through levels of spirit or energetic dimensions), inductively couples with matter. The human being is this force at a foundational level, and it leaves at death of the physical body. But the point is that if this force were ever to leave the human body completely, that body would cease to function in mere minutes. This force sparked conception and powers the presence of who we are in the container we call the human body for its entire sojourn on the earth plane, and when it leaves, we leave with it—because it is our vital life force. We are not here because we have a muscle beating in our chest, pumping life-giving blood to our brain; we are here because a life-giving force resides in our body, allowing that heart to beat and the brain to think.

This primer is a description of how this force operates in the material container (our bodies) that it animates. In other words, this primer is about the reality of how this force has chosen to function in the human body. This is about understanding why we are here on earth and how we operate in this dimension. This is not about religion or a belief system, but rather the truth of how energy is sustained above and below, and how this energetic or spiritual system works unto itself. While this is not a primer about tarot cards, tarot cards are discussed in this primer as a teaching tool to help the reader understand certain realities on a symbolic or archetypical level. The need for this primer is regrettably obvious, for the sources we would normally turn to for trusted guidance in this area are long gone, compromised, or moribund. Those who can understand what is in this small primer will understand, and hopefully those who can't will understand one day.

Being in matter, or should I say existing as a material being, has a responsibility, because what we do materially affects others. And while we are all aspects of Source, we err if we think we can play God or disrespect life. Being on earth may be seen as a game of learning to some, but it is a game with a great deal of responsibility. To disrespect life, no matter how one rationalizes it, is to choose poorly in the game of life.

Lastly, this is not new information, but the desire of my son to have this information made available once more in a more modern way. There will be no "scientific proof" offered here, because there can be no proof of anything outside the third dimension, using third dimensional validations. Some people do not have belief systems that allow them to think outside of the third dimension, and their path needs to be respected for as long as it lasts. But I submit that it is possible to think and feel outside the third dimension. I am grateful to a collective consciousness that is called Rietta Tau Bien, and it was also part of the group consensus that created this primer. Unfortunately, by the end of 2019, the Rietta group was called away from earth on another mission in a galaxy far, far away, and it is no longer reachable. I viscerally went through each law and truth in dream and in meditation, so I am not just a scribe as I was for Galen's *Death Walker* books; nevertheless, it is my hope that my personal experience only added to the clarity of these explanations and did not detract from them.

—K Paul Stoller, MD

PART I

UNIVERSAL LAWS AND TRUTHS— THE LOWER CHAKRAS

Not everything that counts can be counted, and not everything that can be counted counts.

—Albert Einstein

THE FIRST UNIVERSAL LAW - CAUSE AND EFFECT

THE LAW WITH THE LOWEST vibration—the root or most base of the major laws—is the universal law of *cause and effect*. This is the law and truth that reinforces the paradigm of separation: "If I do this, then that happens." It is the law that deals with the very physicality of being incarnate on earth; therefore, it is the easiest to understand and practice. After conception, the very first thing that distinguishes itself in the early developing human embryo, at about week three, is something that is called the primitive streak. The primitive streak will eventually go on to form the central nervous system, but this is the root of the root chakra, and just as with a tree whose roots are connected to the canopy of leaves that touch the sky, roots won't have the same experience as those leaves or even be completely aware of them at all.

It is with the root chakra where separation from spirit[6] takes place.

The unfurling of the little curvilinear embryo opens up into material physical space, and the root causes certain cell lines to follow a sequence. In order for that developing life form to move forward, the cells in it must follow its own form in response to chemical and electric signals. This is all made possible by the law of cause and effect. There is no judgment taking place, only the organization

---

6 The words spirit and spiritual, as well as etheric, will be used multiple times in this primer. Etheric refers to a form or energetic container—a vessel that holds other forms within it, but is outside of the human eye's perception. It is difficult if not impossible to see, except in certain circumstances. For example, one does not see the infrared light from the sun, but one can feel it and see the shimmer of the atmosphere heated by these rays on pavement or in a desert. So, indirectly, one can see the presence of etheric forms under special circumstances. The etheric is a physical presence, albeit outside of third dimensional physical reality, but it is neutral in the sense that it is a field of energy, and while physical it is clearly not composed of elements found on the periodic table. Etheric fields do not hold emotional or mental energy. Spiritual energy holds all of these levels on its plane of reality. It is a different form of a container, a different form of the unseen, a more complete form of the etheric in that sense—but it is impossible to see anything spiritual with third dimensional eyes, though it can be felt. If one does see something perceived as spiritual, it will most likely be an archetype presenting itself so one can relate to it. More often than not it will engage with the emotional field to be perceived. Anyone who has seen something with their feelings will understand this, even though that sounds impossible until you have the experience. It is in the spiritual realm where teachers, helpers, and archetypes exist to communicate with. That is why mental, emotional and physical bodies are all engaged in spiritual connection. Spirit, on the other hand, is that part of self that acts as the link between one's persona and the soul. It is like a dog fetching a stick, but it has a little more intention than that.

of energy in order to create the separate incarnate form. This is why cause and effect become the first development in the human experience. It is also why many have trouble moving past the level cause and effect operates on, because it is so deeply rooted in the subconscious; it is the woven pattern of the human body. The totality of cause and effect is not completely understood until one evolves into the upper chakras.[7] In a sense, the human body is a map to understanding the universal laws and truths.

The spiritual component of cause and effect is to create a framework around which the organization of the human experience can take place, because that organization is needed when moving from the formless into having form in a physical space—something soul[8] and spirit choose to do. But not all conscious beings choose to use incarnate experience and organize energy in this way, and often that is perceived as being a higher path to take, something greater or better than the human experience. Yet the truth is that both paths are equal, even though cause and effect does not apply to this alternative path of development.

Soul agrees to have an experience, and it is the root that grows the structure from which the soul will experience

---

7 Upper chakras are those energy centers (operational transducers) of the heart, throat, brow, and crown.

8 Soul is a level of Source, an expression of Source, that has the capability to stabilize form so it can move into specific arenas—individuation. If Source were the trunk of a tree, the larger roots would be soul families, and the small roots would be over-souls, and the fibers in those roots would be souls. Soul is an integral part of a greater whole.

(not controlling it, but agreed to have the experiences that will await that new body-mind). Certain traditions have assigned the color red to the root chakra, which is the most abundant color on earth and is the easiest to see. But red light does not reveal a lot of detail when compared to the subtitles revealed by higher bands of light. The red ray is also the first manifestation of color in the visible light spectrum.

Many will "file" karma and other religious dogmas, especially the social rules, under this law, and they are connected with the root chakra because the root chakra is about belonging to a structure and system—a family or tribe—in which you have to follow certain agreements. The law of *cause and effect* is about understanding the agreements we are working in. It is also important in that it begins to open up information that leads to *higher laws and truths*, but one has to understand the parameters of separation in order to move past separation. The law of *cause and effect* slows the pace of everything and gives us the time to look at these parameters and agreements, as well as how we are influenced and how we influence others. It works directly with the mind to help it control the ego. The ego is the gatekeeper of separation, after all, for reality to the ego is whatever can be perceived from the root chakra—a place where self-survival is the number one agenda. It is the ego's job to protect whatever mental and emotional mechanisms allow us to survive as a material physical being on earth, at least from the ego's limited root chakra point of view.

The ego should not be viewed as a negative entity. It was present when we were born, for it is that part of us that keeps us "safe"—at least its understanding of safe. It helps us bond with our environment and recognize our limitations (keeping us from doing something stupid on a physical level—well, at least most of the time), so that we can live another day to follow the law of cause and effect. When the ego is unchecked to control the whole life or subconsciously monitors the life without awareness that one can shift and change, then there is an undesirable situation, because that will stifle growth—for example, confusing happiness with receiving instead of giving.

The ego likes things just the way they are, except it always wants to have more influence and control. But growth and change are seen as an anathema. The unknown is to be feared, and it matters not how uncomfortable a person's situation is at the moment. To the ego, an expanded awareness is scary and needs to be avoided. This may not make sense on one level, but the ego does not trouble itself with logic—it is all about short-term preservation, both on a physical level and in protecting all the psychological tools it has gathered to keep us just the way we are.

The law of cause and effect is not just present so you understand that if you do something to someone, they will do something back to you. That is not what it is about. Cause and effect is all about physics. If you interact with energy, that energy will respond in a way that reflects how you interact with it. That is the nuts and bolts of cause and effect. It allows one to move energy in a controlled manner, and that energy can manifest or create. But it is not about dogma or judgment, it is about the ability to understand the very nature of being human as energy and the energy around one, which is why it uses separation and polarity (duality), so it can teach from that form. "If I breathe out, not only does it expel the air from my body, but it moves the air around me as well. If I breathe in, the air expands my body, and I also move the air around me when I breathe in." So, every action creates another action—part of the importance of cause and effect.

Certainly, children learn this law by themselves—if one touches a hot oven door, one receives a painful burn—but the gift of that is it moves the child past the experience of what is taking place in the mind as they see the effect of their actions outwardly into the world. Whether that is about social graces or physical safety—this is a law the naturally occurs—every sentient being understands that when something happens here, something happens there. It is deeply ingrained in the subconscious, which is why teaching someone to slow down and observe—not to be afraid—is a non-trivial matter. But ultimately, cause and effect is here to create an awareness that the next step is to learn how to move the energy around in a focused direction…to manifest. This is the Magician card in the tarot deck,[9] which is relevant, because the tarot deck is a way

---

9 Jean Baptiste Pitois, also known as Jean Baptiste or Paul Christian (1811-1877), was a French author and journalist who developed the modern tarot deck—that is outside of a mystery school. The Magician card is numbered as the first card in the deck of 21 Major Arcana.

to understand universal laws and truths (this is the magic of the tarot). All along someone has put together these laws and truths to provide guidance for the apprentice—a reference point. There is another card associated with the root chakra, but it is held outside the body: It is the card of the Fool, which has a relationship with all the chakras and will be discussed later in the primer.

The law of cause and effect does anchor us into the earth dimension, but because it vibrates at a lower rate, it has been vulnerable to misuse, such as "an eye for an eye" reactions—but that is the dogma part, where that belief is only about possession and identity. While the root chakra is the strongest in the material physical world, it is also the farthest from the seat of consciousness in the human body, so it doesn't pick up on all the nuances connected to higher consciousness—the subtleties of a more expanded view. Being incarnate can feel limiting to something that has been limitless, but being able to expand that incarnate form and blend it with the understanding with higher laws and truths allows for a reconnection to the limitless.

Each law and truth we master on this energetic ladder helps create a maturity so we can keep ascending. And the clearest way to understand *cause and effect* is through the breath[10]—still living life every day, accepting the grace of what every day brings to us. It will teach about

---

10 Especially a guided breath meditation, because it is the outer voice that guides the inner vision that moves one through the cause-and-effect energy field. A live teacher or coach serves even better than a tape or CD, because when it comes to understanding cause and effect, any time two or more are gathered working

cause and effect as it is completely unavoidable on the earth, so unavoidable that many think that is all the world is—"I do this and that happens." The news is filled with stories about cause and effect, so have the discernment not to get lost in the results of it; rather, the focus should be on what all the different parts and players are communicating. There is wisdom in being able to slow the energy down and look at the effect that is happening, as well as the effects you are creating around you.[11]

Cause and effect is a law of low vibration, so it is easy to get lost in both guilt and fear, which are so accessible working with low vibrations. But don't assume you can't have a negative thought without something negative taking place. In fact, the practice of not making assumptions and not taking things personally applies more to the law of cause and effect than anywhere else. When one opens one's awareness into lower vibrations, a natural balance will be available that allows one to be present in these spaces without risking untoward consequences—no need to get caught up in the minutiae.

In each man is the key and the lock. Each man must take his own key to open his own lock. The oil to move the key is loving compassion.

—Old Tibetan saying

---

toward this understanding helps in the appreciation of cause and effect.

11 One person having negative thoughts on one day does not create a war, but they do add to the energy of upset.

THE LAW OF MANIFESTATION

THIS SECOND LAW AND TRUTH is not separate from cause and effect; it is built upon it. The law of manifestation creates the seen from the unseen by bringing spirit and matter together—creating the known from the unknown. The accompanying chakra for manifestation is the sacral energy center that sits in the pelvic bowl, just below the naval, and its orange color reflects the next frequency up on the visible spectrum, picking up more subtle nuances in its higher wavelength then found in the red root chakra.

The law of manifestation is about taking the formless form (chaos) and creating form. This is what the Magician from the tarot deck does—it brings the hidden to be revealed. The power of this law is it gives the "effect" part of cause and effect a platform to step upon from the deep subconscious energy of the root chakra.

The subconscious is in charge of the autonomic nervous system[12], so we don't have to divert the conscious mind to remember to breathe and have the heart beat each and every time. That was the original intention for that subconscious space—allowing the physical body to operate without the need to constantly monitor it. Now, there is actually a monitoring taking place, but the brain does that through electrical impulses and chemical signals. Both intuition and instinct operate in this space, giving the body more information about its environment—not separate from the human experience. But the subconscious helps organize information in the physical experience. When one is asleep, the subconscious rises to the surface, and that is where the conversation takes place with spirit.

Unconscious energy is where the body, mind, and spirit don't know how to organize information, and the unconscious mind becomes a storage place for misunderstood patterns and beliefs—or, for example, past-life experience—so they do not interfere with the physical operation of the day-to-day person. The unconscious can be brought up and worked with, but it doesn't run a silent program in the background the way the subconscious mind does.

Manifestation becomes the deep desire of the human experience, and in the physical human body this is where the organs of reproduction, the organs of creation, are housed—a little below this energy center in the male and a little above in the female. These organs also help play

---

12 The autonomic nervous system controls certain functions of the body, but operates just below the conscious mind.

a role in creating one's identity as well as duplicating that identity. The pelvic bowl is the vessel in which the unseen creates itself (spirit and matter coming together).

The desire to reproduce in the physical is held in the subconscious—to produce something outside of oneself that is a manifested form—so for many there is a desire to have something that is part of self and yet not part of self to continue the manifested form. Therefore, there is a lot of energy that sits in the pelvic bowl—a powerful driving factor for many, sexual energy—but it is also the place where the artist and the actor manifest their creativity. So, duality starts to happen in the second chakra—there is both the creation of a physical child as well as the desire to create something of beauty, music, and art aligned with the spirit—bringing spirit into the physical, but in a different way.

The creativity of the artist rises up and connects with the upper chakras, enhancing them as it accompanies them. The manifestation of a physical child drops down and comes out through the root and then into the physical world—two different streams of energy from the same source. This is not the duality of cause and effect, but the duality in understanding that there are two natures in everyone—both masculine and feminine. So, on top of identity of the root chakra (*"who do I belong to and how do I survive?"*), comes the second chakra's influence on how the individual connects into their physical body and expresses themselves as a male or a female individual.

This is where Source is recognized in the body, because the consciousness expands enough to understand that there is something outside of self that creates, and it is often through the second chakra that one can do the body of work to understand that what is outside is also within. It is where it is recognized that spirit is something that comes up through us and creates itself out into the world. This is where creation is formed.

Manifestation has its own hierarchy, the steps it takes to come to the fore. It begins in spirit and then moves through the mental, emotional, and the physical. Whether it is the creation of a child or the creative manifestation of something that doesn't come through the body—it has to utilize these steps to complete the form of manifestation, which in turn encourages the individual to move up the ladder of energy centers or operational transducer that is the chakra system, to continue to develop, create, understand, and align. That which is created on the outside encourages an understanding of what is inside.

The individual learns that not only are they in the world, but they have the ability to express themselves in the world beyond the need to survive. This is why sexual energy was considered so sacred by certain belief systems—because the connection was made between sexual energy and creation outside of oneself. Spirit comes in as the teacher and uses the creative force to begin to announce itself with the developing human—that first conversation about spirit to matter.

In the tarot deck, the law of manifestation is represented by both the High Priestess, the spiritual form of creation, and the Empress, who represents the physical form of creation. They both hold the feminine, because in the old traditions it was the mother who was the creator. She is the seed, the vessel, the carrier, and the creator on the earth.

> *"Faith goes up the stairs that love has built and looks out the window which hope has opened."*
>
> —Charles Spurgeon

THE LAW OF ATTRACTION

THE LAW OF ATTRACTION IS sometimes called the law of compatibility, depending on one's perspective, but for simplicity it will be referred to here as the law of attraction. It sits in the solar plexus, which anatomically is the stomach and the large nexus of autonomic nerves that lie behind the stomach. But energetically, the solar plexus chakra lies in front of the stomach, just below the sternum, and is represented by the color yellow—a color that can influence color bands both below and above it. The law of attraction acts mutually between two forms, be they relationships between two people, circumstances, or gravity between two or more objects. This law synchronizes them so they will be drawn together to work along the same line of energy—allowing them to be mutual, so there can be reciprocity.

Often the solar plexus is the gateway that allows one to participate in the unified field, which operates beneath the cause-and-effect field. In the unified field all things are connected and all things are possible, which is the way the universe actually operates (outside of polarity); thus, the potential of the solar plexus is to teach about synchronization. In the unified field everything has a right place, right time and is mutually agreed upon in that given space. It is as powerful to understand as it has been powerfully misunderstood, for this is where misuse of *power* can occur.

The solar plexus is the seat of both the ego and the will—that dynamic, driven energy that may try to force compatibility or force attraction. The desire to be rich, covet, or obtain a certain social position is also a part of this, but these are misapplications. All the law of attraction was developed for was to create an attraction for mutual connection—helping those so attracted to resist the sense of separation by the action of being drawn together. The law is activated by the upper expression of the energy coming from the sacral center, creating magnetism in the solar plexus so the desire to create can take a manifested form. And that magnetic field reaches out to the other energy centers and synchronizes with them as well. By drawing two or more forms together, an outer experience can be created that teaches, guides, and aligns.

Many will continuously repeat the same desires instead of letting those desires go out and attract in what serves the highest good for all. So there can be a lot of impatience created in the solar plexus, which in turn can remove one from being centered or standing in one's core, where there is a more universal connection. It can then fracture into separation and limitation, where others are judged by size, shape, color, or social status—a prejudice that does not serve—instead of being the door to understanding that there is no separation. The law of attraction is about learning to both create and align with the life that one lives—a far cry from the way things operate in human society today.

The law of attraction in the world today means you go out and try to possess, instead of having allowance and openness, which is the true energetic nature of this law. Humankind has been out of sync with this law for a very long time. The evolution that is now underway on earth is a transition from the age of the solar plexus into the age of the heart chakra. The age of the solar plexus has been with humankind since hunter-gatherers first settled in communities and became agrarian (seeds planted to attract the energy of the edible plant). But unless the solar plexus can be aligned with the true nature of the law of attraction, there can be a very unbalanced view of the world—a dystopia. Society agreed to exist in the ego-driven solar plexus when the individual was able to take power in their own life, be that tilling their own land, acquiring wealth, or going to war. This goes back to Mesopotamia, and while that lasted a long time, the primitive age of the root chakra lasted millions of years. In between that was the age of the second chakra, when language and art started to develop.

The imbalance of the distribution of wealth in the world today is a direct result of the imbalanced application of the law of attraction, and that imbalance has created a wobble in the matrix that will ultimately bring the age of the heart chakra to the fore. Today, the solar plexus is still very much in control, even though there are many pioneers that are bringing the heart chakra forward. Duality was created in the second chakra, so duality continues into the solar plexus as well. In the tarot, the human version of the law of attraction is represented by the Emperor—the rule of man—and it defines who attracts what along with the distribution of that. The spiritual aspect of this law is represented by the Hierophant. Unlike the High Priestess, who is a keeper of the universal/esoteric spiritual laws, the Hierophant keeps the spiritual laws for presentation and ritual—bringing two energies together, man and God. The Hierophant represents the separation of man from God so they can become mutual and therefore interact.

The law of attraction has been misused, because the human will drives the desire to represent attraction, so one is considered a blessed being, whether that blessing came from God or from a corporation. But obviously, corporations are not godly, and God is not a corporation. Still, in the world today[13], many seem to think they are the same; hence the misuse of the law of attraction. The evolutionary step that is now being taken by humankind is the energy field of the solar plexus. It is no longer the main teaching center in the body, which has now evolved up to the heart chakra—the true seat of power, not the conceived seat of power of the solar plexus. It is not that the solar plexus will not be used, but it will no longer reign supreme in the sense of how humankind will inter-

---

13 2012

act with the environment. The solar plexus seems like it is still in control, but that is out of habit and old patterns.

The law of attraction waits for two mutual objects to come together, much in the same way the stomach waits to be fed. Most people forget that what you put into the stomach determines the health of the entire body—just look at the skyrocketing rates of diabetes and realize that what is being put into the body no longer feeds the body. No longer does the diet most are consuming offer a connection to the earth, and many are generations removed from understanding what is required to grow their own food, let alone the laws of nature, which energetically exist in the solar plexus.

Current events are showing that many "emperors" have fallen and are falling, and even the control of the Hierophant is falling in the eyes of society. There has always been grumbling about what the king or church is doing, yet as they were chosen by God, wealth followed and hence controlled. But now wealth is not a controlling factor as much as it once was. As wealth became concentrated in the hands of so few, it lost its status. And with the loss of status, equalization started to take place. How long it will take for this equalization to be complete is unknown, but most of society is now wise to the manipulation of the law of attraction, and there are many who are striving to bring it into balance, to bring it into mutual connection between two or more objects or two or more people, which will activate the law of attraction. The solar plexus is a very large gate into the ultimate realization that there is no separation.

With the ego as the student rather than the teacher, the right use of it will facilitate an alignment to the wholeness of one's being. And in such a circumstance, the law of attraction really works in an incredible way, because the elements are all in place for it to operate seamlessly. It is a magnetic law, so if ego or will is out of alignment, because neither individual nor community is being served, then the goal is much harder to manifest. Tyrants take control by forcing their ideas on others—but only for a finite time, because their desires are out of sync with the law of attraction. Today, it is very difficult to maintain the illusions that have previously been foisted on society.

Even the technology that supports society has created something that is illusionary, rather than something that is solidly connected to the earth and nature. Faster and more powerful cell phones and computers do not substantially improve the quality of life on earth and the environment around us beyond a very finite point. Understanding the right use of will is part of understanding the solar plexus. Just because you can do something doesn't mean you *should* do it—*does this action support "the highest good for all?" Not just for me, but all?* When you buy something, do you ask how that affects the squirrels in the tree and the air you breathe? Was it made by a quasi-slave receiving unsustainable wages? These are questions that need to be asked, because we cannot separate ourselves from our environment any longer and still be connected.

Often universal laws and truths will be sculpted in the direction of one's beliefs, instead of letting them be the very simple truths that they are. Which is why the solar plexus is the gateway to the upper chakras and spiritual energy. Be it society or individual, one must pass through this gate in a very experiential way, because the law of attraction has to be understood. As to why it opens the gate to the larger truth that there is no separation—it has to become part of one's conscious thought process.

The intuition speaks through the solar plexus, giving that gut feeling or a sense of something in the environment. It can also be judge and jury, which is why guilt sits in the solar plexus and ages the body. So, peace does not happen in the heart, it happens in the solar plexus (especially when one stops trying to control everything in one's environment). The solar plexus supports the deeper sense of compassion by allowing compassion to be understood by the heart chakra, for the solar plexus is the nexus of connection.

THE LOVERS.

THE CHARIOT.

THE LAW OF RHYTHM

THE LAW OF RHYTHM RADIATES the most in the heart chakra, which is the next rung on the ladder up from the solar plexus but is also where the evolution of humankind now finds itself standing—at least at the precipice of the age of the heart chakra. The heart chakra is not like the sacral and solar plexus chakras, both of which have an "as above so below" quality, for the heart is about inflow and outflow in a lateral left and right pattern. So, rather than cause and effect, it is about the pulse and rhythm of the universe.

The heart chakra itself is a master of that rhythm—the beat that fills the chambers with blood, a giving and receiving almost in the same motion. It is why the universal law of rhythm is so very present in the heart chakra, and it is no accident that everything in the body that holds a pulse and a rhythm sits right there around the heart chakra. The heart, after all, is connected to the pulse of the world, and being so connected is the center of power. But in order to hold that power, discernment is required.

One has to understand the give and take of situations and learn to balance that energy, so discernment and balance become the greatest teachers of the heart chakra.

It is out of the ability to see the ebb and flow in events—that rhythm—that one learns how to serve in such a way that is consistent with the highest good for all. When you look at the reactions to any particular situation—the flow of positive and negative thoughts—understand that true power comes with the ability to act, not react. So, in the law of rhythm, if reaction is replaced with discernment instead of judging a situation immediately about whether it is good or bad, then this brings in a balance and the opportunity for a little more connection to the experience. For example, winning the lottery is almost always seen as a positive event, yet someone with discernment will know the excess of money can throw one out of balance—one can lose their center along with the rhythm and flow they had in their life before all the money showed up. There are many stories of those who had a very negative experience after becoming lottery winners, because they reacted to receiving the money, instead of acting to their newfound wealth in a way that would serve the highest good for all.

How may I serve? is the question the heart asks, and it is with that rhythm that the world moves forward. Those who work with their power in this way see the world from a very different perspective. It is true the world seems very polarized at the moment—the haves and the have-nots, some countries being destroyed while others experience growth—at least when seen from a solar plexus point of view. The beauty of seeing things from the perspective of the heart is that you can depend on the energy resetting itself. If it flows out in a negative experience, it will reset itself into a positive rhythm when it flows back in—the yin and the yang. The law of rhythm is often interrupted as the law of karma for this very reason, when a negative experience has to be counteracted by a positive experience, and sometimes it is in the heart where the give and take of karma occurs.

Regardless, the law of rhythm allows the energy to be started again. Much like the blood that circulates because of the pumping of the physical heart, it goes around again and again and again—at least until there is no longer a need to do so and one takes a greater step into circulating their energy in a different way. But the heart never loses that ebb and flow of energy, no matter what form one takes. The law of rhythm is the universal law connected to the heart chakra. It provides a gateway to another level of observation to understand right or balanced action, one's power to choose action with discernment, and one's relationship to the universe itself. It is discernment and balance that give the insight.

The color of the heart chakra is green, as it is the balancing point between the upper and lower chakras and visible color spectrum as well. Sometimes the emotional heart is seen as pink, blending the red of the root with the white of the crown chakra. But as it is the discerning point between the willful yellow solar plexus and the blue of the throat where one actually speaks the next law into existence, it sits there governing that balance. The heart responds to emotional energy and does so immediately. The brain is the only other energy center that gives an immediate response. Of course, the physical heart will beat faster or slower, but the sensation of the emotional heart is where the chest feels full—love, compassion, and connection are felt in the chest. The heart helps these emotions verbalize in the throat, hence the lump in the throat that is sometimes felt.

Physiologically, the heart has a direct connection with the emotional body through the vagus nerve, which makes connections with physical, emotional, mental, and spiritual bodies, and the heart responds immediately to the chemical and electrical messages conveyed by that nerve. The vagus nerve innervates ear, throat, lungs, heart, and stomach, so on more than one level this is how the brain gets its messages out to the rest of the body. But it is the heart that allows messages from the unseen and intuitive worlds to be perceived by the body using the very same nerve. So if one needs to let intuition and instinct come through, the vagus nerve gives it language, although the information itself comes into the body through the crown chakra and the pineal gland. Nevertheless, between heart and solar plexus is the clearest perception for intuition and instinct available in a human body, and this the place where discernment transforms hate and fear into love and compassion, thus changing the state of that which is being perceived. It is the heart that interrupts and brings the information in preparing to give it a voice in the throat chakra.

Of course, there are those who get caught up in the emotional heart, who do not know how to feel and can't make the decisions to take a choice—they can't see the rhythm and therefore need the guidance to back up into the observer self (the most refined aspect of the personality, which tends to be much more neutral). For example, an exercise that can help would be to become conscious of a calm breath going in and out in a moment set aside for contemplation. Feeling the heart beat in the chest, knowing how the heart actually functions, provides some insight into how to be with the heart chakra and the law of rhythm. When you can relate to something on a physical, emotional, mental, and spiritual level, then instinct and intuition will fill in any missing piece, even if the mind doesn't fully get it.

It is through the heart chakra and the law of rhythm that the records of the soul's activities are accessed—the Akashic[14] records. In the tarot deck, two cards represent the law of rhythm and the heart: the Lovers and the Chariot. The Lovers card is not about sexual energy or even about coupling. It is about choice, seeing the balance and flow of masculine and feminine energies and channeling them through discernment to bring forward the heart's calling—*How may I serve*? This card depicts male and female in union, because they come together—the universe comes together in that energy field to become One. So, the Lovers card represents the emotional heart.

---

14 Galen referred to the Akashic hall of records as the Hall of Cups in the Death Walker series.

The Chariot represents what power is—a human driving two horses, one black and one white (polarity), that have to pull together—move in unison to move forward. It recognizes one's ability to harness the ebb and flow as well as act, not react. It is about manifesting—not a new car in the driveway, but being a master of the energy that is present in the moment and having the discernment to know how to serve in that space. The law of rhythm puts one in service and in power—*How may I serve?* is about making a choice about how to live, and moving in a direction that is *in the highest good for all.*

This is about the compassion of the open, outstretched hand—seeing oneself as more than a mere object, but as a master of the universe, because living openhandedly puts one in alignment with the flow of the universe. The driver of the chariot knows he is not in complete control of the horses, that there has to be a third element involved. Everyone has to understand the rhythm and the language (forward, stop, left, right), so the wise charioteer knows he is not in control as much as in the flow. So, while the Chariot card is about choice, it is also about being in balance with those choices.

Green is a prevalent color on earth because earth is a heart planet. It is a teaching ground of polarity, and if one masters that polarity (not control it, but is with it), it happens through the heart. Also, the vast majority of the higher life kingdoms on earth have a heart, because there is an agreement that there is an organ that acts as the central core that would be the heart of the matter, so the say—bringing two halves together to create a whole.

THE HERMIT.

STRENGTH.

THE LAW OF VIBRATION

The law of vibration is home in the throat area—the throat chakra. Yet everything vibrates—even so-called inanimate objects are vibrating. It isn't so much about motion as it is about the placement of that object harmonically in space-time—occupying many places at once, because reality is taking place on multiple levels. So things vibrate, because there are multiple shifts of energy taking place between the numerous levels of reality being occupied—the more levels being occupied, the more vibration. The law of vibration radiates—up, down, and side-to-side, but it is not just engaged when someone is using their throat or vocal cords. It is engaged all the time. Speaking isn't part of what the throat chakra does, but what it does do is hold a harmonic frequency, and it vibrates on the in-breath and the out-breath—making manifest the energies of all the chakras below it.

The energies of the lower chakras vibrate up and come out through the throat chakra, so when you hear a human voice, no matter what is being said, all the qualities and intentions of the other chakras come through and ride upon that voice. The intentions of the individual come through in the harmonics, not the way the words are pronounced or their content. The information that comes from this chakra holds all the information about the body it belongs to.

There is a hierarchy of manifestation—first, the pure light from Source, followed by color, which holds the intention of that light, and then sound (vibration). So, it is the law of vibration that takes light and color and converts it into sound, making the throat chakra a primary gateway to harmonize the physical, emotional, mental, and spiritual forms. In fact, all the major chakras are a gateway, which means they provide a very particular path to follow. But the throat chakra is the universal door to manifestation; whether one can speak or not, manifestation moves itself through that chakra.

The organ the throat chakra sits in front of is the thyroid gland, which regulates energy utilization in the body and energetically holds the emotion of hope. Hope seems like a very subtle emotion, but it often makes the difference between health and illness. Even if one is already sick, if hope and positive thought are held, the body heals faster. Color is the cradle of intention, and the color of the throat chakra is blue—a very available color that has the broadest and most even frequency on the visible spectrum. It is easy for the human eye to see blue, but above that frequency it becomes much more difficult for color to be seen. As well as projecting outward, the throat also receives, and teaching information from spiritual realms often comes on the blue ray of energy into the throat.

The law of vibration is fundamental to understanding manifestation, but it is also fundamental because it helps provide an understanding that everything is in motion—everything is shifting and changing in the flow of life. The tarot card pair connected to the throat and the law of vibration are Strength and the Hermit. Normally, the Strength card is about an individual overcoming their animal nature, and the artwork on this card often depicts the human demonstrating that they are stronger than the animal or subconscious mind. But truth and love are the strength of the universe, and strength comes from all the loving intention that is gathered in the body and moves forward out into the world. Often there will be an infinity sign depicted on the Strength card, which is another representation of the law of vibration—the eternal movement of up, down, and side-to-side.

The Hermit card is not about isolation or separation, but about the sage/warrior—the way-shower who has found enlightenment in the dark and has found balance of light and dark, thus conquering polarity. The Hermit shows the way through the perceived imbalances to a balanced state. The Hermit is often seen as someone who has taken a vow of silence, which only points out that the throat chakra is not about the spoken word as much as the intentions behind those words. The Hermit is the teacher of experience, and many times when the truth is spoken, that in-and-of-itself creates the bridge, excites the energy, and shows the intention.

The way to understand the law of vibration is to remember that everything vibrates—nothing is still. The heart is about discerning what action to take next. The throat chakra lines it up to create what the heart desires—the harmonic of manifestation. The practice of toning, singing, voice reminds one that the human body has its own harmonic that comes through in the vibration of the vocal cords. There are many mantras that can be used, including the simple word of manifestation on the third dimensional plane—Om. The practice of toning helps bring the energies that flow in the body to the center—the masculine/feminine, the solar and lunar channels, the heavens and the earth.

WHEEL of FORTUNE.

JUSTICE.

THE LAW OF GENDER

IT ALMOST GOES WITHOUT SAYING that the law of the masculine/feminine principals is misunderstood, for it has nothing to do with sexuality or even separation of the sexes (found in the sacral chakra). The law of gender has everything to do with completely merged masculinity and femininity. Everything in reality applies the masculine and feminine principals to keep the *light* and the forms light takes moving forward—not unlike the yin and yang, where one pours into the other to create the motion of the universe. The masculine principal is about outward movement and the force of will. The feminine principal is about inward movement—observation and intuition. When they unite, they create forward movement.

Like a seed, the law of gender allows everything to grow out of it; even the atomic structure shows the play of masculine and feminine principals. Rather than light being some mysterious energy (neither wave nor particle), it moves itself into the material world by stepping itself down a notch—through the exchange created between electron and proton. In this universe, everything is light in one form or another. But the difference between the law of manifestation of the sacral chakra and the law of gender, as it relates to the human body, is the *glands* involved.

The law of manifestation has the gonads to express itself through for the most part, but the law of gender has the pineal gland and the pituitary gland and seats itself in the core of our physical CPU—the brain. These two glands create the masculine and feminine features in a material human body. So the brow chakra, the third eye, by bringing the masculine and feminine together, sees the cohesiveness, the separation, and the wholeness within any given quantum of anything. It is in the brain that the law of gender keeps flow in the generation, regeneration, and creation cycle. Now, as this law flows down into lower chakras, it slows itself down and helps create a physical separation of the sexes, so the principal of gender is seen all through the physical form. But in the unseen world, this law is the spark that moves life forward and is not slowed down by just expressions in the physical world. Masculine combing with the feminine principal is the light that keeps life ignited—it is the eternal flame of creation. From there color, and then sound, all move forward under the power of this law.

The pineal gland organizes the masculine and feminine, and the pituitary activates the integration of these principals for the brow chakra. If one were to imagine a line from the brow to the base (or nape) of the neck, that line would intersect these two glands, and this is the flow of energy from the brow and out the base of the neck, where it circles around into the throat chakra, giving this manifest form. There is an energetic zig-zag pattern of this life force—the flow between all the chakras is not just a straight line from crown to root. The flow of life force in the body actually uses the law of gender as it moves back and forth to connect with the energy centers in the body.

The color of the brow chakra is blue-violet or indigo. The crown chakra, the energy of which flows forward into the brow, is often depicted as white but is actually ultraviolet. The tarot cards associated with the law of gender and the brow chakra are the Wheel of Fortune and the Justice card. Traditionally, the Wheel of Fortune card was seen as being about one's fortune and how the energy spins to determine one's fate. But the truth is this card is about masculine and feminine principals being applied—the observation of will and introspection that turns the karmic wheel and changes the fate, eventually allowing life to be viewed as a wheel rather than a line of energy that goes from birth to death. It holds the truth of generation/regeneration and creation in that wheel, and where the observer sits on that wheel is where the information comes through. The brow chakra, the all-seeing eye, is part of the Great I (Am), in the sense that *I am* is the masculine principal and *me/myself* is the feminine. In the brow chakra, the observed and the observer come together.

The second card is Justice, which should speak for itself, but most think this is about punishment. This card represents a position where all things are seen, balanced, and allowed. (Allowance in this context is that balance takes place with permission having been given on some level, because justice cannot happen unless permission is given.) And it is the balance of the two cards that creates the law (of gender), and with that understanding of this balance, light itself is activated. So, while justice implies judging, this is about compassion and not the harsh determination of right and wrong. The Justice card is about making sure the universal laws are applied with loving compassion to keep the scales balanced, allowing the observer and the observed to work cohesively with one another. The masculine and feminine principals unify to work with each to other create balance in the physical, emotional, mental, and spiritual forms. It is of interest that in the Major Arcana of the tarot deck, the Justice card sits in the middle of everything, just as the pineal and pituitary glands sit in the center of the brain.

In way of review, polarity is where the masculine and feminine principals, the dark and the light, do not recognize each other—there is no conscious recognition of the energy—and it can take a great deal of work on the part of the observer to bring those two halves together. With the law of gender, they naturally occur together and work together to create balance, and that spark sets things in motion in both seen and unseen worlds—just like an atom that naturally has both proton and electron self-contained and acting in accordance with one another to emit light and energy. The law of gender is the representation of unison, where masculine and feminine have merged and cannot be pulled apart from one another.

Under the law of gender, the light and the shadow are the same, and the energy is unified and the same on every plane of existence. It is the final attunement of the law of cause and effect (polarity), the ultimate form of masculine and feminine that does not separate itself. Polarity, on the other hand, does not exist in all dimensions—it exists on the earth, which is why so many come to earth to understand the law of polarity, where masculine and feminine can operate independently of each other. It is only the observer that unifies these two principals through the third eye to understand them on a universal level. If there were a tarot card of the hermaphrodite, it would belong to the brow chakra—but that is not a tarot card.

THE LAW OF UNIVERSAL MIND

Sometimes known as mentalism, the law of universal mind rules the crown chakra. Everything in the universe is mental in the sense that it organizes itself into a perceivable form, and it is *thought* that creates experience from what is perceived. So light, color, and sound are formless until they are organized and become geometric form and then archetypical form, which is not only the hierarchy of manifestation, but everything that is perceived. It comes through the crown chakra and gets organized along these lines into the mental, emotional, and physical body, and then one's experience is created out of that through *thought*. This law is about the passage of the formless into form—not manifestation, but organization. Above the law of the universal mind is the *uber* law of no separation. The unified field sits in the mutable energy of that law, which oversees all the laws and perceptions below it.

There is a difference between mind and universal mind. The mind is the last to know, for it only knows what it has been taught; it does not perceive outside of its experiences. But universal mind does. The law of universal mind allows a conversation to take place between mutable and immutable energy, as will be explained.

Now, the only reason the soul bothers to incarnate is for experience—without that, it remains in an open-energetic space, which is just fine for the souls that choose to remain in that neutral open pool of life force—a neutral space in the sense that it doesn't organize itself down into perceptions, ideas, or forms. It is only when the universal mind pours itself through that organized portal called the crown chakra that it experiences. All the universal laws and truths discussed in this primer are consistent for all, yet they are still perceived differently through each person's persona. Of course, this makes it difficult to explain universal laws and truths beyond their consistency and how they seed themselves in the human experience.

The universal laws are solid and unswerving, just as an acorn will always grow into an oak tree—never a squirrel or a turnip. They are consistent in the way they are experienced, but perceived differently in the way each individual interprets their experience with them. The energy of the universal mind that comes down through the crown chakra transceiver is pure and neutral. It has no agenda or conceptions—it is simply seeking form, so it is mutable. Once in the human body, that energy is organized in such a way so that it can learn from, perceive with, or judge by a perceptible experience. When that individual sends that energy back up and out the crown, such as in meditation, it has all of those connections to it. It has been imprinted by that individual's intention. It is now immutable. This is how one can transmit healing energy to another, by drawing in the neutral energy of the universal mind and then breathing it back out with the intention to heal or harm, to create or destroy.

It is a responsibility to be in a material body, for that body will create experience. And while that is the only reason anyone becomes incarnate; the created experience does impact others. The universe is teeming with life, and as there is no separation, it matters not whether one lives on a deserted desert island or a crowded city; one's experience impacts the whole of life.

The crown chakra is designed to be open. At birth, in a very practical way, it is literally open, which allows the infant to move through the birth canal. It remains open and a sensitive area for many months, connecting the child to the formless chaos from which it came until the body can align, design, and perfect, understand, create, and motivate that fontanel bone and the energy of that body into a particular patterns and forms.

The crown is the fulcrum to the higher chakras (not to be confused with the upper chakras of heart, throat, brow, and crown). If you were to imagine an equatorial triangle inside of which was a human body seated in a lotus position, fitting nicely into such a triangle, the crown chakra is connected to another equilateral triangle that is inverted, and in it is a flipped mirror image of that individual that completes the chakra system into the etheric body. It is somewhat like the infinity symbol, but obviously more angular. The crown chakra in that inverted triangle is actually the evolved root chakra of the etheric body, and the whole system of the lower and upper chakras reverses itself in the reflected higher chakras.

The human experience may seem to be a purely third dimensional operation, but just as third dimensional objects cast a second dimensional shadow, the same holds true for forms in the fourth dimension—they will cast a third dimensional shadow. The inverted triangle of the higher chakra system is the fourth dimensional form of the human experience, and it casts it shadow into the third dimension, being the lower and upper chakras and the physical human body that is animated by them.

In the evolved root chakra (the higher crown), the tribe becomes the whole of energy, and its theme is not about survival, but connection to that wholeness. It completes a course of energy by allowing the root, which is the lowest vibration in the physical body, to become the highest vibration in the etheric body, thus allowing a completion of a cycle of physical and spiritual energy. The point of mentioning this is that as one connects to each chakra in the physical body, one can draw a line to the corresponding higher chakras above and complete a circuit of energy, thus aligning physical and etheric chakras so that the energy field is completed in the body. This would give one access to more energy and information and to different perceptions than that of the five senses. It would allow one to access information from their trans-dimensional self.

The color of the crown chakra is twofold. The part that is connected to the scalp is violet, but the radiant point right above that is white. So, the fulcrum of the chakra system between physical and etheric bodies is represented by the white light just above that physical body. In that narrow band of white light is the most expansive and clearest form of Source that is available; it holds unimaginable levels, layers, and worlds within that space. It is akin to the event horizon of a black hole, because once you begin to go into that point, there is no turning back. In the process of passing out of the material body, once one (the spirit) moves past that balancing or zero-point, there is no return back into that earth body. This is also the point of contact between the universal perfected pattern above the physical body and that point of transformation to another cycle of experience (so-called death).

Those who weave the chakras together in meditation and ascend up to the crown find it is very difficult to move past the crown chakra without experiencing the wholeness of *no-thing*, where the law of no-separation exists (zero-point). This is the state of Samadhi or Nirvana—that open space where everything can relax and align. But just above that is the mirrored perfected pattern that on rare occasions some healers can bridge to realign that perfected pattern back into the physical form to strengthen and clarify the earth body. It is a crossroads of change where one understands what direction life is asking one to go in. This is the portal where light, color, sound, geometric form, and then archetypical expression come into the body to work directly with the persona of that individual. This is also where space-time is experienced. Often this is a place beyond reason, and the scientific mind cannot go past this point. To put it simply, past this point the third dimension is left behind, and there can be no scientific proof of anything beyond the third dimension.

The life force that comes into the transceiver of the crown chakra is the only endothermic force of nature that exists in the third dimension; in other words, it does work with producing heat. The chakra system is an array of secondary biological operational transducers that orient the energy as a wave guide and focal plane, so that the energy is constructively mediated by the consciousness or thoughts of the body it is operating through. This trans-dimensional energy life force or zero-point field is the source of our origin, for it is Source. It is where we came from and will return.

The most profound teaching in the tarot is to understand the two cards connected to the crown chakra. The Hanged Man and Death are the cards of the crown chakra—the most powerful cards and undoubtedly the most misunderstood, for it is bringing the mystery of the universal mind into a more organized explanation.

The Hanged Man is hung upside down by one foot on the tree of life. It is not about sacrifice or crucifixion, but it speaks to the beginning of the inverted pattern of the higher chakra system, where the top of the etheric head touches the top of the physical head. It is also a card of enlightenment. Without that projection of light forward and the understanding that this system continues above the physical body (that there is more than what the mind thinks), one can *hang* in limbo, for there is no understanding that there is a whole universe of mental form that helps create, design, and allow each individual personality to organize its own experiences. The unenlightened truly hang in limbo, for they only understand the experiences, patterns, and perceptions of what is in the physical world. They are not open to the universal mind and all the knowledge and understanding that flow in through that inverted pattern, channeling down into the physical form, and that physical life does look like sacrifice, karma, and crucifixion from that limited perceptive.

The Death card represents the door or gate one must go through to release the physical form as being the only teacher, reality, or existence available. As one releases that, one transcends death by understanding that there is no death. This card then represents a portal where the formless seeks a form to create itself with. This card is all about the release of the fear of death. Sure, the material body dies and flesh recycles itself, but above the material earth plane there is freedom of movement where there is no limitation. Usually, this card is a skeleton riding a dark horse, trampling or fascinating the individuals around it. But when you understand this on a different level, the horse is about will and choice, and the rider upon it expresses how it will walk through that door. So that takes on a different meaning beyond suffering and the end of the physical body—it is about letting one's understanding open up to the very bones of that experience.

Mentioned earlier, the Fool card also has a place here, because it represents the un-manifest going into manifestation. It is an unusual card, because it can fit wherever it is needed to help understand the experience. It has no number assigned to it, so it is meant to be a neutral experience. It represents the prodigal son in the sense that as it takes a step, it gathers tools, experience, and understandings. This is what incarnate experience is about—ultimately returning to wholeness and returning to Source (the World card—the end of the journey that begins again).

THE LAW OF NO SEPARATION

IN THE WHITE LIGHT OF the top part of the crown chakra, the balance point between dimensions is present, and this is where the presence of Source is focused most intensely into the human experience. This is the place where the law of no separation is most understood—in other words, just above the law of mentalism. Remember, everything in the universe is mental, for it has to perceive, conceive, and create. At that white point of light, the law of no separation expands to cover everything above and below. It radiates to the higher chakra system and radiates down to the lower and upper chakras—it is the overriding foundational law and truth for everything in this universe.

No separation is the law and truth from which all the others derive their foundation, because it is the thread of truth through which everything flows. In that sense it is not even appropriate to give it a number in the hierarchy; it is a sun, and all the others are but planets. Yet despite being primary, it has confounded many who have tried to appreciate how there can be *no separation* when we physically see separation with our eyes and when we can feel that separation with our bodies. Yet, there is a shared vibration that moves through everything in our benevolent universe, and while there are many other universes in the greater cosmos, this truth is what applies in our benevolent universe. It moves through light, color, and sound, which are the three elements that bring together every form, every galaxy, and every atom that we will ever come across. It radiates through the physical, mental, emotional, and spiritual realms—keeping them cohesive and in communication with one another.

Everything around us is in communication with us. That alone should create understanding of *no separation*, because everything is in relationship with us. And what this particular law and truth does is help release the sense of isolation that is felt by so many. The human mind has gotten used to the idea of being separate, and it responds or reacts out of that, even though half of our consciousness (the subconscious) is moving in rhythm to this universal truth. Our cells respond, our body temperature responds—everything responds on the subconscious level. All of our subconscious thought processes are in relationship to no separation.

The reason this is the primary universal law and truth is because once it is understood, then all of the others are very evident to the conscious mind. But it is primary because it comes from Source unaltered and runs deep as a radiant pulse in *all* that is present in this universe, both physically and energetically.

If this primary law and truth is not appreciated, how does one begin to perceive it? Understandably, there has been a lot of dogma built up around this. Some will say you can only perceive it through prayer; some will say you can only perceive it through belief; but the beauty of a universal law and truth is that whether you perceive them or not, they still exist. Science, and especially physics, already has figured out that there is *no separation*. After all, our own physical bodies are made up of stars; the atomic material that our human bodies are made of was literally created in stars and will be recycled one day just as it has been recycled—nothing in this universe is new. There is no thought or form that is brand new that isn't standing on the shoulders of something that was already there, and even stars that are being born today are made up of materials from older stars that have died. There is always a recycling of form.

If we can understand this on one level, then it is not hard to appreciate that nothing begins or ends. As one form rises, another form dissipates; it is the cycle of creation and destruction. It is possible to develop a practice of openness to understand this full circle of energy—receiving and releasing. Even paying attention to the breath will start an understanding of this rhythm. The breath comes in and releases out, and when it is released, it is changed. But then the next in-breath begins that cycle anew. It can be with this simple exercise that an understanding of *no separation* will occur.

For most of us, this understanding must come in through the mental body[15] and perceived through the mind that there is *no separation*. Once that understanding occurs, the body starts to remember and starts to communicate on a different level, which is called the unified field, where one can literally swim in the pool of *no separation*. Each movement responds to the next, each thought responds to the other, and everything is in harmony, with no limitation to the energy field that one is surrounded by. This can be tapped into when in a meditative space (whatever that means for an individual)—an expanded field in the mind, in the body, and in the breath. It is another way to perceive that there is *no separation*. But this particular law and truth has to come through the mental body first, and be invited—in that sense of belonging or connection.

This law and truth do not carry the dogma that if you are good enough or smart enough you will understand it—nor is there a deity that has any claim over any universal laws and truths. Dogma cannot exist in these spaces. They are timeless. They just are.

Here is a mundane example of this law and truth in action. Imagine one has a problematic and disrespectful neighbor who makes a lot of noise and throws their trash over your fence. The dogma of that would say that if there is *no separation*, this neighbor represents an aspect of yourself; therefore, you must be the one with the problem, which the neighbor is reflecting back to you. But that is not necessarily a truth. It may just be an opportunity to

---

15 As has already been pointed out, the mental body is not the mind, but a universal bridge of thought and intention.

practice forgiveness by realizing your neighbor is doing the best they can do at their level of understanding and allowing you to work with this in a different way at your level of understanding. Dogma would have one pull this all onto oneself—judging yourself because of the actions of others. That actually creates separation, when the truth is found in doing what is required to harmonize one's environment. Once that is understood, the situation will often align and open, because there is nothing more to observe and nothing more to learn from that experience.

This was an oversimplification with numerous exceptions, but the point being made is that the events are not always what they seem to be, and the observer in us—the *observer self*—by applying the law of *no separation*, can see the neighbor as acting out the destroyer cycle of release—just the same as what an out-breath symbolizes. And if you don't draw attention to it, the situation will balance out. Granted, that can take a level of maturity many do not possess, but holding that perspective or philosophy will bring to the fore a more unified field to work from. When one can understand the connections and communications that take place all around us, there is a delight in just tuning in to the natural world—the signs and symbols of communication. For example, one need look no further then the often ignored crop circle symbols that now exceed over 5,000 worldwide, for they are replete with messages and meaning from a highly intelligent source utilizing the earth itself to communicate.

The observer self can bring what we encounter in our environment into the unified field without judgment—

just by seeing that there is a certain flow of energy. So while the experience to understand a universal law and truth can take lifetimes, the description of these laws and truths is not lengthy.

It is human nature to try to possess and own things, to try to make things uniquely our own. It has to do with the root chakra—*if I have it, then I can survive it*. But there is no "owning" something that says nothing is separate from anything else, and therefore access to the universe is available to all. Once this law and truth is absorbed and understood, you can see how reality would be perceived as being in constant communication with us, be that through dreams or intuition. Now, because this is a primary truth, it is often the most challenged truth: "How can you say there is no separation when this happens or that happens and an entire population of humans stands independent from one another, not knowing what each other is thinking or doing?"

So, no separation is the most challenged law and truth, only because it is the most misunderstood one. Once that challenge has been addressed, the other universal laws and truths come to the fore. Ultimately, it comes down to understanding why a soul chooses to incarnate on earth, because earth is where one tries to understand these laws and truths. The conundrum is that it is not possible for the human mind to appreciate what a soul is; nevertheless, it can acknowledge that an aspect of Source that is called the soul chooses to utilize a path to participate with the earth, and that you are that path. And the purpose of such an effort is to be under the influence of the earth's main operational paradigm or field, which is the field of polarity or duality. Along with duality comes a profound sense of isolation and amnesia about where one came from and one's identity.

There isn't any other way to put this, but without participating in the perceived separation, isolation, and amnesia, many of the experiences the earth has to offer would not be possible—no one would not want to play the "game." However, there comes a time when there is a desire to move past the main lesson plan and participate in a more conscious manner with what is offered on earth. After all, the unified field is also available to participate with and brings with it a whole new set of experiences that the soul can utilize from the earth dimension.

There is no set formula for how the human experience learns to grow, balance, and reconnect with the wholeness that is part and parcel of the unified field. But it will find the best combination to serve that end under the larger law and truth. *Having said that, there are those who clearly understand what the law of no separation means. Therefore, it is by no means an impossible task to integrate it into one's scope of awareness.*

PART II

THE HIGHER CHAKRA SYSTEM

THE UNIVERSAL KEYS

THE ETHERIC BODY AND THE higher chakra system create a perfected pattern that stabilizes the physical body connected to it. The chakra system is a ladder, but it isn't always organized as one. When the transition is made to the other side, there is no chakra system, because one becomes the whole system as chakras merge with one another. This is why views and experiences are organized differently on the other side than they are in earth physical bodies. Even so, the chakras are still utilized, because the human vessel is still present to organize and communicate with.

TEMPERANCE

The higher chakras do not hold color, so they do not radiate with violet or blue any more than UV light or X-rays that are above the visible spectrum hold color. The inverted crown chakra, the higher crown, which sits in the upside-down triangle right above the crown chakra of the material body, has a different role than the crown transceiver that opens up a portal to receive thought from the universal mind. The higher crown is a step-down transformer—a funnel. It takes all the energy above, all that universal form, and in a spiral fashion steps it down, so by the time it reaches the end of the funnel, it is prepared to move into the hierarchy of manifestation—light, color, sound—and integrate with the physical human experience at the level of the crown chakra. Paradoxically, stepping this energy down actually speeds it up, much like a marble would speed up as it spirals down a funnel. From there it is deposited into the crown as the creative spark of life itself. In that sense, it is both Alpha and Omega—the beginning and ending points of the whole chakra system

The higher chakras do not need to be activated, as they are already fully active, perfected patterns. One can't influence them, but their purpose can be understood. One can sit with the crown chakra energy and interact with the chakras below, but one can only be with the higher chakras and allow them to teach about their purpose and how that purpose integrates with the human experience. So the higher crown is a spiral that speeds up and delivers. The spiral is a universal symbol for movement, and also for a portal. The higher chakras have only one tarot card connected to them that can assist in understanding the quality of these chakras, and the card of the higher crown is the card of Temperance.

Traditionally, the Temperance card is that of an angel pouring water from one vessel into another, which is what the higher crown does—it brings one level of energy contained in an etheric vessel and deposits it into a physical vessel without transmutation. It may be concentrated, but the energy is delivered as it was created above. This energy is the same spark of universal force that hits physical matter and brings it to life during conception. It is the purest form of energy in the universe, and just as in the Temperance card, the water does not change as it is transferred from one vessel to another. Temperance is about moderation and self-restraint when accepting the energy from above, as it often has to be moderated and come into a different language where restraint is required as it trickles into the form below it. But it is also a card asks the individual to utilize the resources available in a more expansive way through the process of moderation and restraint. That is the part to be mastered, because one needs to truly understand the information to pour it into another vessel. That is where temperance is a universal teacher.

This angel pouring water from one vessel to another while standing solidly on the earth is the only archetype that can represent this truth, and an exercise to help understand temperance is to just visualize this archetype and be with it.

THE CROSSROADS

Following the inverted higher chakra system up is the higher brow or third eye, where the soul decides what will be utilized in the incarnate life of the physical being below. Decisions about what form that physical body will take and what it will be working with both challenges and grace. Of course, it has a great deal to do with the DNA of the physical body. But DNA isn't everything, and epigenetic issues, or those factors that control the expression of DNA, can drastically change the physical experience for an individual. Another decision that is made at this level is what experience from past lifetimes will come to the fore to be utilized or organized into the current lifetime in a physical way.

The chakra system of the physical body (lower and upper) is oriented along a vertical axis, but the higher chakras of the etheric body spin horizontally, akin to an x axis. The brow in the physical body tends to be about foresight and intuition. What is being viewed is often the etheric field information of the higher brow chakra—genetics, past lives, and all of those intentions that have set themselves into motion for the physical form. One is not fated to just be those intentions, for one remains open to learn from the experience those intentions help create. So one's incarnate life is not a fixed reply of old experience, unless the individual's free will and choice deliberately try to experience a do-over—which is never really possible, because circumstances are never the same twice. The intention is not to destroy the physical body, as one might think if the decision is made to have some debilitating disease, but to make the individual stronger.

The geometric symbol of the higher brow is an equal sided cross, because it is literally a crossroads: A decision is being made in agreement with soul as to the experiential opportunities being created for that incarnate life. The tarot card this chakra works with as a teaching tool is the Devil card. A controversial figure to be sure, but traditionally the Devil card is about temptation and understanding how to balance the physical experience with the energetic—the inner and outer world. It is also about what form one takes—animal versus spiritual, or some of each. Many shamans see both their shadow and their light and utilize both their physical form and their energetic form to create and understand from.

The Devil card isn't about evil but about the mastery of the shadow and the light, and how that utilizes the maximum level of experience on the earth plane. So at the level of the cross in the higher brow, one decides which direction one is going to go in. And it is not about which direction is chosen but understanding how one is walking their path. Traditionally, the tarot card of the Devil actually depicts the pagan goat-headed deity called Baphomet—and goes even further back to Pan.

Sitting in the higher brow can help clarify a path—decisions made before entering the incarnate space and the decisions that are at hand in the physical space.

THE CONNECTION

Just as powerful as the throat chakra is in the physical body; that is how powerful the etheric throat chakra is in the perfected pattern above the physical. The higher throat chakra sets the framework of the emotional life and how one accesses emotions—how one will perceive and feel and utilize their intuition. It is the throat chakras (physical and etheric) that anchor and hold the emotional body. The higher throat sets the emotional tone for one's life. A family can have five identical children, but each one will experience life differently on an emotional level, because choices of emotion will be different from one child to the other and influence the emotional experience of each child differently. There are those who will be very open and sensitive with a very developed emotional body, while others will use other tools to regulate their lives. But it is the throat that connects one to the physical body, and regardless of how one expresses their emotional body, that body is very important in how one connects emotionally in the physical experience. So, in the hierarchy of manifestation—spiritual, mental, emotional, and physical—the higher throat is what energetically connects one to the physical body and is very important in being able to express, connect, and bridge—regardless of how much or little one utilizes their emotional body to experience life on earth. The drop of soul force, life force, that descends into the funnel of the etheric body spends some time at the higher throat determining just how it wants that incarnate form to emotionally interact with the environment, and how that persona will display their emotions, such as masculine versus feminine. These choices stabilize in the higher throat.

Healers who have an ability to access this energy center can learn what that body is working with on an emotional level. The geometric key for the higher throat is the triangle, pointed up for masculine and down for feminine, so this key can help express that polarity for the individual. The triangle is the only universal key that will show polarity and can be used to show the emotional quality of the lower chakras belonging to the individual below. The tarot card connected to the higher throat is the Tower, a card depicting a structure that is breaking apart from a lightning strike. Now, when one is very clear with their emotional body, and information is flowing from the physical to the mental without obstruction, then illusion will be removed—and that is what the Tower card is about. It destroys the structures of illusion that one perceives oneself to be, so whatever that belief is about self, something may come along in life to remove that illusion. For example, if someone thinks they are a coward, a situation may come along that asks them to be heroic. The Tower card helps the higher throat by disassembling illusion so the emotional body is free to operate.

The higher chakras do not carry the personality's trauma; the whole etheric body is a neutral zone, but it will prepare the lower chakras to work with energy in its purest form. Once again, the tarot card is used as a tool to understand the quality of what the higher perfected patterns hold. The etheric body does not hold illusion and doesn't really hold polarity, but it helps channel into the physical body a quality of energy to be utilized in experience where there is polarity and illusion. And the Tower card helps break down the structure of illusion—it is designed to create revolt and revolution, destroying old structures so new structures can begin. This is all about being in the emotional body, and the health of the physical body is directly determined by the health of what is taking place in the emotional realm. Just a reminder… emotions are not what you feel; they are only the expression of the emotional body.[16] The beauty of the Tower card, while it may be frightening on one level, is that it absolutely means one has come to the end of an old structure, and everything will change from that point on.

Many are now feeling this, because so much energy is being built up into the heart chakra that it is forcing the throat chakra open. Many are in crisis mode, but the Tower card signifies for them that change is at hand as more illusion is cleared.

---

16 The emotional body is that energetic conversation between spirit and matter. It may not be verbal, but it has to converse and translate that conversation in some way. So, the expression of the emotional body is the feeling that one has; however, the quality of that feeling can be influenced by the mind, so the feelings one has may not be clearly the expressions of the emotional body. The emotional body is just energy waves that radiate through the physical body, and it can take practice to just tune in to the true nature of a situation without other interference. Illusion can certainly muddy the waters, as well as transference from other experiences that do not apply to the current situation. The emotional body is also the bridge to the mental body—the conversation of the universal mind with the physical body.

THE DECISION

With each step higher in the etheric chakra system, these energy centers have less to do with the development of the persona and more to do with soul, along with light, color, and sound—the universal manifestations of Source. The high heart is the last center that has a connection with the persona, compared to the centers above the high heart, which is represented by a circle, the representation of a universal teacher. It is in the high heart that the decision to complete conception occurs, to go forward and carry out the agreement to incarnate. It is the gate where the decision to become physical manifests itself. It isn't about what that manifestation is going to look like or feel like, it is just about the decision, yes or no: "Will I continue with conception or release the experience."

Once the decision is made to bring that full spark of conception into physical form, agreements and contracts accompany that conception. This is the heart of the matter, the reason one even bothered to incarnate. Of course, the answer will be to have experience and bring a consistency to contracts, agreements, and the experiences that were decided upon. "I will be in my heart, or I will not be in my heart." A simple yes or no, and that is what the high heart is all about.

The tarot card that accompanies the high heart is the Star card. Often it depicts a woman or an androgynous figure that holds two vessels of water. One vessel pours into a body of water, and the other pours the water onto the earth. The Star card is about possibilities, hope, and trust—in a sense, it is about the structure of those agreements and contracts. It doesn't define whether they will succeed, it doesn't define if the water poured on the ground will grow anything, or if the water being poured into the larger body of water will raise the level of the larger pool of water. Nothing is for sure—it is just a card of opportunities and possibilities. It creates a balance between giving and receiving, which is what the physical heart chakra does as well. None of what is spilled out is wasted. Every action has a purpose and a reason behind it.

When one agrees to come forward into the physical by the action of conception, one also agrees to have certain structures in one's life (this is not about fate)—certain agreements, so that they can be utilized to develop, create, and understand. In other words, coming into incarnation is not random, and yet it is random enough to allow free will and choice. For example, in one life an individual may have been a talented singer, but in the next life their vocal equipment was not the best, so they were not pulled into the life of a singer. The randomness is that anyone can sing, but this individual is not directed into that talent, because other contracts and agreements are in place. So, even though they sing and may love music, life doesn't take them down that path again, because they may have learned all they can learn from that particular form and their next life is about different agreements.

Of course there are always exceptions, for if the stars call for it—pun intended—even a very unattractive individual with a gritty voice can become a famous singer. The wisdom of the high heart is so clear that the wisdom and humor of the universe can be seen in the most unlikely situations. In the physical form, the heart is literally the rhythm of life, and life is always unpredictable. In the etheric, the heart is about the rhythm of choice and that true agreement to be present and in the physical life, which makes the high heart perhaps the easiest etheric chakra to relate with, because there is always a conscious connection to it. The high heart is the last gate where once a decision is made to incarnate, the persona and all the chakras below have to develop and formulate, so that individual can move into the physical form.

THE TRUST

The high solar plexus is represented by the square, which represents a physical teacher (a teacher with a little more personality than a universal teacher). It works in combination with the high heart, even though the etheric heart is the gateway where the decision to be born happens.

The high solar plexus helps gather back the individuality to view the wholeness before the decision is made to reincarnate in the high heart. It draws the energy together, much as a sculptor would bring together wet clay before deciding what to turn it into. It starts to individuate that energy so the aspect of the soul that will come into physical incarnate experience is not just sitting in the soul's intention. Since the soul is the sculptor, here the contracts and agreements are drawn together, as well as the new unique mind and persona, so the high heart has something to look at and decide whether it wants to agree to this or not.

The etheric solar plexus is not as personable as the high heart, because that is actually what is developing in the high solar plexus, and the tarot card associated with this is the Moon card. This card is unique, because it about the higher forms of intuition—universal intuition, in the sense that it is about understanding the reflection of what is taking place on a universal level. If you can understand what the purpose is of everything—the rhythms and the connections—it is where the symbol comes into the conscious form. But it is the rare person who is comfortable with the shadow and the light of themselves and being able to trust in the next step without knowing what that next step is. So many look to the moon and its reflective light to shine upon something so it can be recognized. But the interesting thing about moonlight is it can create a completely different image than what sunlight can reveal. So it is about the intuition clarifying what lies in the shadows and complements that individuality. Each individual needs assistance in seeing past their own diversions. The light of the moon is not enough to see clearly, and intuition alone does not give one clarity at what they are looking at, because what one intuits doesn't always play out as it was intuited.

The Moon card is about trust—just because you can't see something doesn't mean something negative is taking place. In the process of individuation there is an innate trust of everything universal, spiritual, mental, emotional, and physical. That trust is what gathers that individuality together in the high solar plexus.

THE JOY

The next two (first two etheric chakras) have nothing to do with the personality. They are just portals and gates. They organize energy, but they don't have anything to do with how the personality will work with it.

The final two have very unique symbols linked to them—the high sacral chakra is the pointed oval created by two overlapping or intersecting circles coming together—spirit and matter coming together in wholeness creating another level of manifestation, the Divine female and male energy combined together to work in harmony with everything that circles below it. It is the beginning of separation but still combined in a unified form—still androgynous. This is represented in the tarot by the Sun card, the simple recognition of joy in union symbolized by the universal laughing child on a pony, the simple emotion of joy, of beingness in the openness of existence in this benevolent universe. This love and joy is represented in the high sacral chakra.

The universal laughing child is aligned with its will, represented by the pony it rides upon—being able to sit upon it in innocence and connectedness, living as if everything is a garden and everything is available right there with no want or need—just that experience of being. This card represents living wide awake and living openhandedly in the container that is the body. Truly, pain and suffering are not a part of the desired agreement.

THE JOURNEY

The high root chakra is about the beginning of the journey and is represented by a shining star, for this is where light, color, and sound come together to create a manifest form for the aspect of soul that comes in and begins to manifest with that light, color, and sound. And it is that simple—purity unto itself. In the tarot deck this is represented by the Judgment card, which signifies resurrection and forgiveness of the past. Calling everything forward to renew itself in that cycle is referred to as reincarnation. Traditionally, this card is depicted as an angel calling the dead out of their graves; it's as simple as that. Whatever cycle or circuit that happened before renews itself in this new particular life experience—very pure.

THE BEGINNING AND THE END

Floating above all this is the etheric form of the Fool card, which while integrated into the physical chakra system, stands on its own as well. For the higher chakras, this card is the World card, which is really the resurrected fool. The Fool card often works with the lower root chakra, but the World card is represented by a figure that is dancing in a circle of laurel leaves, representing a competed form and moving into a completed form. It is the Alpha and the Omega. It is the same motion as the fool stepping off the cliff, but it does so with great awareness. Both the World card and the Fool card are wild cards, as they are not connected with any one chakra, but they influence them all. It is the prodigal son in the sense that it is the journey of the personality through spirit and matter. The World card is more the angelic form of the fool, where the fool is more the very physical youth—just different levels of the same form. This is the real Death card, because it represents a completed form choosing another cycle of death and rebirth.

So ends the universal primer and the twenty-two cards of the Major Arcana from the tarot deck used to describe the energetic system.

ABOUT THE AUTHOR

Galen Stoller was in many respects an all-American kid. He liked going to theme parks and movies, visiting his grandparents, hamming it up at school, and hanging out with his friends. Steeped in the world of sci-fi/fantasy, he read the complete Harry Potter series, the Golden Compass/Dark Material series, and the Bartimaeus Trilogy. He also read the C. S. Lewis Narnia series over and over, except for the last book, in which all the protagonists were killed in a train accident—a volume he read once and never wanted to return to.

It was a train accident that would take Galen's earth life when he was sixteen years old. At the time, Galen was in eleventh grade at Desert Academy in Santa Fe, New Mexico, and starting to think about enrolling in college. An accomplished actor, he was about to perform the dual roles of Fagan and Bill Sikes in *Oliver!* He was an ethical vegetarian and helped train dogs for Assistance Dogs of the West. Because of this service, he was nominated posthumously for the 2008 Amy Biel Youth Spirit Award. Following the second anniversary of his passing, he asked his father to start writing *My Life after Life*, the first book in what he called the Death Walker series.

ABOUT THE EDITOR

K Paul Stoller, MD, started his medical career as a pediatrician and was a Diplomat of the American Board of Pediatrics for over two decades. Previously, in the early 1970s, he was a University of California President's Undergraduate Fellow in the Health Sciences, working in the UCLA Department of Anesthesiology and volunteering at the since disbanded Parapsychology Lab at the UCLA Neuropsychiatric Institute. He matriculated at Penn State and then completed his postgraduate training at UCLA.

His first published works, papers on psychopharmacology, came to print before he entered medical school. During medical school, he was hired to do research for the Humane Society of the United States and became involved in an effort to prohibit the use of shelter dogs for medical experiments, which made him very unpopular in certain circles when he published an article entitled "Sewer Science and Pound Seizure" in the *International Journal for the Study of Animal Problems.* He was then invited to become a founding board member of the Humane Farming Association, and served as science editor for the *Animal's Voice Magazine*, where he was nominated for a Maggie Award.

In the mid-1990s, after a friend, the head of Apple Computer's Advanced Technology Group, lapsed into a coma, Dr. Stoller began investigating hyperbaric medicine. Soon after, he started administering hyperbaric oxygen to brain-injured children and adults, including Iraqi vets and retired NFL players with traumatic brain injuries, also pioneering the use of this therapy for treating children with fetal alcohol syndrome. He was granted a lifetime Fellowship in the American College of Hyperbaric Medicine.

When his son was killed in a train accident in 2007, he discovered the effectiveness of the hormone oxytocin in treating pathological grief.

www.ingramcontent.com/pod-product-compliance
Lightning Source LLC
Chambersburg PA
CBHW072057290426
44110CB00014B/1722